POKE!
THE SEA URCHIN
AND OTHER ANIMALS WITH SPIKES

Greg Roza

PowerKiDS
press
New York

Published in 2011 by The Rosen Publishing Group, Inc.
29 East 21st Street, New York, NY 10010

First Edition

Editor: Jennifer Way
Book Design: Kate Laczynski

Photo Credits: Cover, pp. 1, 20–21 Frederic Pacorel/Getty Images; pp. 4, 5 (top), 10, 14, 16 Shutterstock.com; pp. 5 (bottom), 6, 17 iStockphoto/Thinkstock; p. 7 Jupiterimages/Photos.com/Thinkstock; p. 8 Digital Vision/Thinkstock; p. 9 Ace Kvale/Getty Images; p. 11 (top) © David Courtenay/Peter Arnold, Inc.; p. 11 (bottom) Tim Laman/Getty Images; p. 12 Jean Tresfon/Getty Images; p. 13 Tobias Bernhard/Getty Images; p. 15 © Chris McLaughlin/Animals Animals-Earth Scenes; pp. 18, 19 (bottom) Jason Edwards/Getty Images; p. 19 (top) Ted Mead/Getty Images; p. 22 Hemera/Thinkstock.

Library of Congress Cataloging-in-Publication Data

Roza, Greg.
  Poke! : the sea urchin and other animals with spikes / by Greg Roza. — 1st ed.
      p. cm. — (Armed and dangerous)
  Includes index.
  ISBN 978-1-4488-2552-3 (library binding) — ISBN 978-1-4488-2688-9 (pbk.) —
ISBN 978-1-4488-2689-6 (6-pack)
  1. Animal defenses—Juvenile literature. I. Title.
  QL759.R69 2011
  591.47'7—dc22

                                    2010028524

Manufactured in the United States of America

CPSIA Compliance Information: Batch #WW11PK: For Further Information contact Rosen Publishing, New York, New York at 1-800-237-9932

CONTENTS

OUCH!

Millions of years ago, dinosaurs walked on Earth. Many of them were giant and did not have to worry about **predators**. Others had strong plates to **defend** themselves. Some dinosaurs used thick spikes to defend themselves. For example, stegosaurus (steg-uh-SOR-us)

The thorny devil is a lizard that has a body covered in sharp spikes.

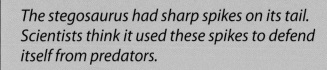

The stegosaurus had sharp spikes on its tail. Scientists think it used these spikes to defend itself from predators.

had long, sharp spikes running the length of its tail. If a predator got too close, it might give it a nasty slap!

Modern animals have many ways to defend themselves from predators as well. Just like the stegosaurus, some are armed with spikes. Get too close, and they will poke!

Sea urchins, like the ones shown here, have spiky bodies. In many kinds of sea urchins, these spikes are poisonous.

Have you ever seen a cactus? It is covered with sharp spikes. Few plant eaters are brave enough to take a bite out of one. Those spikes hurt when they poke! Some wild animals also use spikes to defend themselves. A spiky animal does not generally make a good meal because it can be hard to swallow!

Cacti, like the ones shown here, are covered in sharp spikes. The spikes give a painful poke to animals that touch them.

Some spikes are large and thick. Others are long and thin. However, all spikes poke and hurt! Some animal spikes, such as those belonging to many sea urchins, have **poison** in them. The poison can make an animal sick. It can even kill an animal!

STAY BACK!

The spikes on a porcupine's body keep it safe from other animals. Predators or curious animals need to get poked only once before learning to stay away from porcupines for the rest of their lives.

Animals with spikes use them as **weapons** to defend themselves. They poke their spikes into a predator's body, breaking the predator's skin and causing pain. Animals have different ways of using spikes. When a predator gets too close to a porcupine, the porcupine turns its spikes in the predator's direction. The predator might run into the

Porcupine quills stick in the skin and are painful to pull out. This dog got too close to a porcupine and now has a face full of quills.

spikes, or it might get poked trying to bite the porcupine.

Some animals, such as the sea urchin, are almost totally covered with spikes. They do not need to move at all. Anywhere a predator tries to bite, spikes are waiting to poke it!

OTTERS AND URCHINS

Spikes cause pain. This helps an animal defend itself in two ways. First, the pain comes suddenly and causes a predator to stop attacking and run away. Second, predators that have been poked remember that pain and think twice about trying to attack that animal again.

Sea otters dive under the water to eat all kinds of animals. However, they are one of the few animals that eat spiky sea urchins.

They will likely even teach their young to avoid animals with spikes! While spikes are great at keeping most predators away, some animals have figured out how to get past them. For example, sea otters know exactly how to eat sea urchins. They flip the urchins over and bite them where the spikes are much shorter.

On the underside of a sea urchin, shown here, the spikes are shorter. It is easier for the sea otter to bite into the sea urchin there without getting poked.

SEA URCHIN

Sea urchins have hard, round bodies. They can be many different colors. All are covered with long, sharp spikes, though. They also have several **tube feet** that they use to move around on the seafloor. These tube feet have suckers and sharp teeth that sea urchins use to defend themselves.

The spikes of many sea urchins are poisonous. If a

The seafloor in False Bay, in South Africa, shown here, is home to many different kinds of colorful sea urchins.

This fish tried to eat the sea urchin shown here and now has some of the urchin's spikes stuck in its mouth.

predator attacks one of these sea urchins, the spikes pierce its skin and send poison into its blood. The spikes can also break off in the predator. The poison causes pain. Numerous spikes can cause weakness, **paralysis**, and even death.

PUFFER FISH

Puffer fish are not good swimmers. They move slowly and are easily caught by predators. However, they have a special way of defending themselves. Puffer fish can quickly suck water into their bodies and make themselves big and round. It is hard to eat a big, round, spiky balloon!

Some puffer fish are covered with spikes, which makes them extra hard to

When the puffer fish is not blown up, most of its spikes lie close to its body.

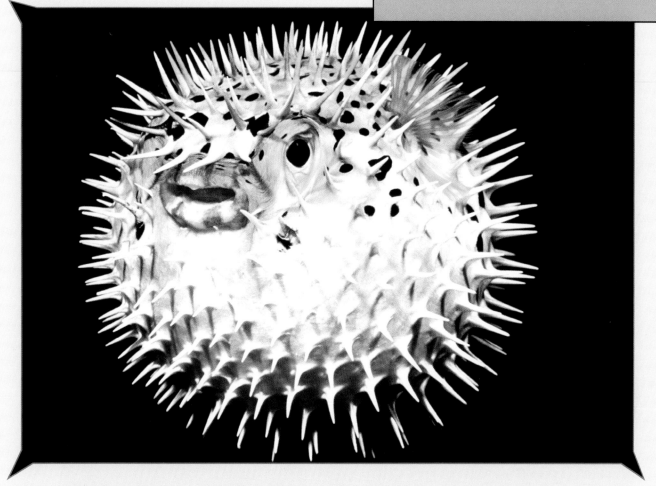

When the puffer fish is blown up, as this one is, its spikes stick out all over its body. They are ready to poke any animal that comes near it.

catch and eat. Puffer fish pose another danger. Many of these fish are poisonous to eat. The poisons in these puffer fish's **organs** can cause paralysis. They can also stop a predator's lungs and heart from working.

PORCUPINE

There are about 24 kinds of porcupines. All of them have spikes called quills. The quills on a porcupine's back, side, and tail normally lie flat. When the porcupine senses danger, the quills rise up!

When a porcupine is relaxed, its quills lie flat and close to its body.

People once thought porcupines could shoot their quills, but that is not true. However, the quills fall out easily when touched. They often stick in a predator as it runs for cover. The end of a quill has **barbs** on it. This makes it hard to remove once it is stuck in a predator's skin. Porcupines grow new quills to replace the ones they lose.

THORNY DEVIL

Thorny devils are lizards. They have colors that help them blend in with the sand and rocks of the Australian deserts where they live. When a predator is near, a thorny devil stands still and is very hard to see. The lizard can also tuck its head between its legs to

The thorny devil can stand very still. Its coloring helps it blend in with the desert around it.

show its false head, which is a spiky bump on its back. Predators mistake the false head for the real one. This gives the lizard a chance to escape.

Thorny devils also have spiky bodies. These hard, sharp spikes make some predators think twice about trying to eat the thorny devil.

The Australian bustard is one of the few animals that eat thorny devils.

FUN FACTS

1 Sea urchins might be spiky, but that does not stop some people from eating them! They are often eaten raw, without the spikes.

2 Sea urchins are closely related to sand dollars, sea cucumbers, and starfish. They are all members of a group called echinoderms, which is Greek for "spiny skinned."

3 The red sea urchin can live for up to 200 years! This is the longest-living animal on Earth.

In Japan, fugu, or puffer fish, is a very expensive dish. Specially trained cooks are needed to prepare the fish because if it is prepared wrong, it can kill! In fact, many diners die of puffer fish poisoning each year.

4

One porcupine can have as many as 30,000 quills.

5

The thorny devil uses its spikes to defend itself. It has another use for them too, though. When it rains, the spaces between the spikes guide rainwater to its mouth.

6

DON'T GET POKED!

Every year, many people step on poisonous sea urchins when they walk into shallow waters where the animals are resting. Some people pick up urchins, without knowing what they are and how poisonous they can be. Sometimes divers pick them up by

mistake. Sea urchin pokes can be very dangerous. They often get **infected**.

Porcupine quills are not poisonous. They are very painful, though. Porcupines can leave hundreds of quills in a person. If you ever come across a porcupine, back away as quickly as you can.

GLOSSARY

barbs (BARBZ) Sharp spikes with hooks at the ends.

defend (dih-FEND) To guard from being hurt.

infected (in-FEK-ted) Had an illness caused by germs entering the body.

organs (AWR-gunz) Parts inside the body that do jobs.

paralysis (puh-RA-luh-sus) Loss of feeling or movement in a part of the body.

poison (POY-zun) Matter made by an animal's body that causes pain or death.

predators (PREH-duh-terz) Animals that kill other animals for food.

tube feet (TOOB FEET) Water-filled, strawlike parts on some sea animals that are used for moving. They are open at the bottom.

weapons (WEH-punz) Objects or tools used to hurt or kill.

INDEX

WEB SITES

Due to the changing nature of Internet links, PowerKids Press has developed an online list of Web sites related to the subject of this book. This site is updated regularly. Please use this link to access the list:
www.powerkidslinks.com/armd/poke/